Original title:

Moonbeams and Pillow Dreams

Copyright © 2024 Creative Arts Management OÜ

All rights reserved.

Author: William Hawthorne

ISBN HARDBACK: 978-9916-90-516-6

ISBN PAPERBACK: 978-9916-90-517-3

Radiant Petals of the Night

In the hush of evening light,
Petals bloom, a stunning sight.
Whispers soft on gentle breeze,
Nature's calm puts hearts at ease.

Stars above, they wink and nod,
Underneath, the earth stands odd.
Moonlight bathes the blossoms bright,
Painting shadows, pure delight.

Fragrance dances through the air,
Colors rich beyond compare.
In this garden, dreams take flight,
Radiant petals of the night.

As dawn approaches, colors fade,
Yet in hearts, the beauty stayed.
Memories of a starlit scene,
In our minds, forever green.

Wandering through a Twilight Realm

Footsteps soft on twilight ground,
Whispers of dusk all around.
Shadows stretch and colors blend,
In this space where night descends.

Paths wind through the dusky gloom,
Crickets hum a nightly tune.
Trees stand tall, their branches sway,
Guiding dreams that drift away.

Stars appear, like jewels bright,
Dancing gently, pure delight.
In this realm where time stands still,
Wandering hearts seek their thrill.

Beneath the veil of twilight's grace,
Hope ignites in every place.
In shadows cast, new stories start,
In this realm, we'll never part.

Fantasies in the Stillness

In whispers soft, the night unfolds,
A tapestry of stars, stories retold.
Hushed breaths weave through the silent air,
Fleeting moments, dreams laid bare.

Shadows dance beneath the moon's glow,
As time drifts gently, moving slow.
Wishes linger on the edge of dawn,
In stillness, hopes are drawn.

Tranquil Moments of Rest

The world lies down in quiet grace,
While sunsets paint a tranquil space.
Softly sighs the evening breeze,
Carrying whispers through the trees.

A blanket of stars, a soothing sight,
Cradles the dreams that take to flight.
In this embrace of night's caress,
We find a moment, pure and blessed.

Enchanted Nocturne

Beneath the veil of twilight's song,
Magic weaves where hearts belong.
The moonlight glimmers on the stream,
Painting paths of silver dream.

Crickets chirp a lullaby,
As shadows stretch and softly sigh.
In the arms of night so kind,
Enchanted moments intertwine.

Radiant Dreams of the Night

In the stillness, dreams ignite,
Radiant visions, pure delight.
Stars above in silent gleam,
Cradle us in a gentle dream.

Each heartbeat echoes through the dark,
A symphony, a hidden spark.
In night's embrace, we find our flight,
Radiant dreams, our guiding light.

Gentle Caress of Darkness

In the velvet hush of night,
Stars whisper secrets, taking flight.
Shadows dance with graceful ease,
A soft embrace in twilight's breeze.

Moonlight drapes a silver veil,
While dreams weave stories, sweet and frail.
The world slows down, a tender sigh,
As twinkling gems adorn the sky.

Hidden Hues of Sleep

In a realm where shadows blend,
Dreams are colors that transcend.
Whispered thoughts in slumber's grasp,
Elusive visions gently clasp.

Softly flows the tranquil stream,
Woven deep within our dream.
Every hue a silent song,
In this calm, we all belong.

Ribbons of Light and Dreams

Awakening with morning's breath,
Life unfolds, escaping death.
Ribbons of light stretch and sway,
Warming hearts in golden play.

Chasing shadows from the night,
Hope ignites with newfound light.
Dreams take flight on gentle wings,
In the joy that daylight brings.

Night's Quiet Canvas

Across the sky, the colors blend,
Night's canvas breathes, inviting friends.
Stars are brushes painting bright,
A masterpiece in the still of night.

The moon dips low, a guiding eye,
Soft whispers flutter, an age-old sigh.
Each moment captured, time stands still,
In the silence, the heart can fill.

Comforts of the Dark in Glittering Echoes

In velvet shadows, whispers creep,
The night unfolds, secrets to keep.
With every heartbeat, calm and low,
Comforts of dark, a gentle glow.

Stars flicker softly, stories untold,
In the embrace of night, the brave, the bold.
Through silver streams, the dreams take flight,
Echoes of solace in the depths of night.

Starlit Gardens of Forgotten Fantasies

Beneath the moon, a garden lies,
With starlit blooms and whispered sighs.
Forgotten tales in petals sway,
As night unveils their secret play.

In twilight realms, imagination grows,
Among the leaves, lost dreams compose.
Where wishes dance in silken light,
Starlit gardens bloom in the night.

Threads of Light in Night's Tapestry

Woven in darkness, threads so bright,
Stitching together the fabric of night.
Glimmers of hope in shadows cast,
Embroidered moments that ever last.

Each twinkling star, a meaningful line,
In night's vast quilt, where dreams entwine.
With gentle hands, the heavens weave,
Threads of light that we believe.

Lanterns of Imagination in the Stillness

In the hush of night, lanterns glow,
Guiding the heart where thoughts can flow.
Stillness cradles the mind's escape,
Imagination's flight, a wondrous shape.

With gentle flames that flicker bold,
Stories unfold, both new and old.
In the quiet dark, our dreams are spun,
Lanterns of hope, till night is done.

Celestial Whispers in Slumber's Lullaby

In the hush of night, dreams softly sigh,
Stars weave stories in the velvet sky.
Moonlight drapes the world in silver sheen,
While shadows dance in a tranquil scene.

Whispers of angels cradle the night,
Guiding lost wanderers with gentle light.
Each heartbeat echoes in the stillness around,
As the universe hums a soothing sound.

Night's Silken Embrace of Stardust

Wrapped in night's tender, silken shroud,
The whispers of stars gather like a crowd.
Dreams take flight on wings of pure bliss,
In the quiet realm, where magic exists.

Softly the moon spills its luminous tears,
Washing away all the fading fears.
Hearts entwined in a celestial dance,
Lost in the rhythm of a timeless trance.

Nocturnal Murmurs Beneath Starry Veils

Underneath the blanket of shimmering night,
Nocturnal murmurs speak soft and light.
The cosmos hums in melodic tone,
As shadows linger, no longer alone.

Stars blink secrets in the quiet air,
A language of love, both tender and rare.
As dreams bloom gently like flowers in spring,
In this serene moment, our souls take wing.

Dreams Adrift on Lunar Light

Drifting on beams of the moon's soft glow,
Dreams unfurl gently, hidden below.
Each flicker of light holds a world to explore,
As visions entwine on the cosmic shore.

Lost in the tapestry of night's embrace,
Lunar reflections illuminate space.
A whisper of hope in the stillness blooms,
As night wraps around all the shadowed rooms.

Twilight's Dance of Serenity and Night

As daylight fades into shadows,
The stars begin their gentle glow.
Whispers of the evening breeze,
Carry secrets only night knows.

The moon casts its silver embrace,
Enfolding the world in calm light.
Dreams awaken with soft sighs,
In the dance of serenity, delight.

Crickets serenade the twilight,
Harmony in each fleeting sound.
Nature's lullaby surrounds us,
In this refuge, peace is found.

Listen closely to the silence,
It speaks volumes in the dark.
A symphony of still moments,
In twilight's tender spark.

Distant Shores of Dreamlike Illusion

Across the waves of the unknown,
Where reality meets the surreal,
I glimpse the shores of my visions,
Where dreams and desires reveal.

Soft sands kissed by foamy tides,
Hold the echoes of long-lost tales.
Each footprint tells a story,
Of wanderers and their sails.

The horizon melts with the sky,
Blending colors in a soft swirl.
A canvas painted by the heart,
In the dance of a dreamer's world.

Here the heart can freely wander,
Untethered from the daily grind.
In distant shores of illusion,
Magic awaits, unconfined.

Chasing Reflections in a Silver Pool

Beneath the willow's graceful swing,
Ripples dance on mirrored glass.
Chasing dreams that drift like clouds,
In this tranquil moment, they pass.

The moon dips low to share its light,
Painting silver on a quiet face.
The water holds a realm of wishes,
Where time stands still, a sacred space.

Casting stones, I watch them sink,
Creating circles, fading fast.
Each reflection tells a secret,
Of shadows, legends from the past.

In this pool, I find my heart,
As whispers weave through gentle lulls.
Chasing reflections, I discover,
The beauty that within me pulls.

Soft Glows of Enchanted Slumber

In the hushed embrace of night,
Dreams arise like fireflies' light.
Cocooned in warmth, the soul takes flight,
Soft glows wrap the world in delight.

Moonlit fairies dance on dreams,
Whispers of magic fill the air.
Each lullaby in shadows gleams,
As fantasy unveils its fair.

Time drifts slowly, a gentle stream,
Where all is peaceful, soft, and sweet.
In enchanted slumber we gleam,
Nestled in dreams, we feel complete.

Awake to dawn, a tender kiss,
Where dreams of night gently fade.
Yet the echoes still exist,
In hearts where magic's always played.

Mystical Mornings Await

Softly dawn breaks the sky,
With hues that whisper and sigh.
A gentle breeze starts to dance,
Nature's call, a sacred chance.

Golden rays filter through leaves,
Where every heartache believes.
Footsteps tread on dewy grass,
Embracing moments that pass.

Birds waltz in cheerful flight,
Painting the canvas of light.
In this realm, dreams intertwine,
Awakening spirits divine.

Mystical mornings unfold,
Tales of wonder retold.
In the hush of new days,
Where magic forever stays.

Glint of Fantasy

Through the trees, secrets gleam,
A world alive with a dream.
Fairy lights flicker and glow,
In the twilight's warm, soft flow.

Magic dances on the breeze,
Whispers carried with such ease.
In this realm, wishes take flight,
Guided by the stars at night.

Colors burst in vibrant hue,
Painting skies with dreams anew.
Moments caught in joyful spin,
Where the soul can truly begin.

Glint of fantasy, so bright,
Igniting hearts with pure delight.
In shadows where the stories play,
Imagination leads the way.

Starlit Whispers in Bed

In the stillness of the night,
Whispers gather, soft and light.
Under blankets, dreams unfold,
Starlit stories gently told.

Pillows cradle each sweet thought,
While the world outside is caught.
Moonbeams kiss the quiet space,
Dreamers find their sacred place.

Voices made of silken sighs,
Echo softly, like the skies.
In the hush, hearts intertwine,
Filled with warmth, your hand in mine.

Starlit whispers softly weave,
Magic found in what we believe.
In the dark, our dreams align,
In this moment, love will shine.

Ethereal Quilts

Wrapped in layers, soft and warm,
Ethereal quilts, a soothing charm.
Threads of dreams sewn, night by night,
In their embrace, hearts take flight.

Patterns dance in twilight's glow,
Stories woven, long ago.
Each stitch a tale, each patch a way,
Memories held, where spirits play.

Whispers linger in the seams,
Softly spoken, like sweet dreams.
In quiet corners, peace will dwell,
In these quilts, our hearts can tell.

Ethereal comfort, soft as air,
Stitched together with tender care.
Underneath the night's embrace,
Find your solace in this place.

Frail Fantasies in Moonlight

In shadows cast by silver beams,
Whispers dance like fleeting dreams.
A world of soft and gentle sighs,
Where starlit hopes too often rise.

Beneath the glow of night's embrace,
We wander through this mystic space.
With every glance, a story told,
In memories of dreams so bold.

The moonlit path, a silken thread,
Where half-formed thoughts and wishes tread.
Each flicker sparks a reverie,
Awakening what's lost at sea.

In frail fantasies, hearts take flight,
As secrets weave in velvet night.
A fragile glow that fades at dawn,
Yet lingers on, though dreams be gone.

Secrets of the Night Blossom

In twilight's hush, the petals sigh,
Revealing secrets hidden nigh.
A fragrance sweet hangs in the air,
As stars emerge with gentle flare.

Beneath the canopy of dark,
Life stirs in shadows, leaves a mark.
In night's embrace, we find our way,
To where the heart and dreams can play.

The moon's soft touch on velvet skin,
Awakens longing deep within.
Each whisper holds a timeless song,
That carries souls where they belong.

In mystery's fold, the blooms unfold,
With tales of love and joy retold.
They flourish in the night's caress,
Revealing secrets, we confess.

Dreamcatcher's Lullaby

Moonbeams weave a tender spell,
In silence, dreams begin to swell.
With every breath, a wish takes flight,
Guided by the gentle night.

Softly whispers, lullabies hum,
As shadows dance, and echoes come.
The world, a canvas, painted bright,
By dreamcatcher's soft, woven light.

In realms where fantasies are spun,
Hope ignites as day is done.
Each fragile thread, a tale aligns,
Embracing hearts as starlight shines.

Through whispered sighs, let troubles fade,
In tranquil peace, deeper shades.
Hold tight to dreams, let worries cease,
In timeless flow, we find our peace.

Embrace of the Dusk

When dusk descends, a soft caress,
The world relents, finds sweet recess.
In purples deep, and golds that blend,
A quiet moment to transcend.

The sky, a canvas filled with grace,
Holds the promise of a sacred space.
Where twilight drapes its velvet hue,
And whispers warm, like morning dew.

Embrace the hush of fading light,
As stars awaken from their flight.
With every breath, the night will bloom,
Dispelling shadows, banishing gloom.

In the arms of dusk, we rest our fears,
With quiet thoughts, we shed our tears.
In stillness found, our hearts ignite,
Together held in soft twilight.

Gentle Tides of a Nighttime Ballad

Whispers of the ocean call,
Underneath the starlit sky.
Moonlight dances on the wall,
As soft breezes gently sigh.

Waves of silver kiss the shore,
Melodies of night unfold.
With each crest, our spirits soar,
In the warmth of tales retold.

Dreams drift like clouds above,
Carried on the tides of time.
In the stillness, feel the love,
Swaying to the ocean's rhyme.

Close your eyes and drift away,
Let the lullabies begin.
In the night, we find our play,
Gentle tides, a sweet, soft spin.

Beneath the Cosmos' Embrace

Stars awake in velvet night,
Whispers of the cosmos call.
Glistening in radiant light,
As the universe enthralls.

Galaxies spin, a waltz divine,
Infinite in their grand design.
Beneath the heavens, dreams align,
In this vast and sacred shrine.

Comets trace a silver line,
Linking worlds we may not see.
In this dance, our souls entwine,
Bound in cosmic harmony.

Hear the silence, wise and deep,
In the stillness, find your place.
Beneath the stars, our hearts will leap,
Lost and found in love's embrace.

Shadows of Lullabies in the Twilight

In the twilight's gentle glow,
Shadows stretch and softly sigh.
Lullabies begin to flow,
As day whispers its goodbye.

Crickets chirp a sweet refrain,
While the sky adopts its hue.
Memories like falling rain,
Dance in dreams awaiting you.

Candle flames flicker and fade,
Casting warmth on weary hearts.
Night's embrace, a tender shade,
In this world, all pain departs.

Drawn to twilight's soft caress,
Settle in, let worries cease.
In these shadows, find your rest,
Sleep will bring the soul its peace.

Radiance in the Realm of Sleep

In the realm where shadows play,
Radiance softly glows.
Dreams unfold in bright array,
Filling hearts with gentle prose.

Among the stars, we take flight,
Floating on a silver stream.
Endless wonders beckon night,
Inviting us to chase the dream.

Every thought a spark divine,
Crafting tales in slumber's hold.
In this magic, hearts align,
As we weave our dreams of gold.

Drift away on clouds of light,
Let the night cradle your soul.
In the radiance of twilight,
Feel the warmth, let love be whole.

Reflections in a Darkened Room

Shadows dance upon the floor,
Whispers echo, memories soar.
A flicker of light, soft and dim,
In this silence, I feel him.

Glass frames hold the past so tight,
Capturing moments, lost in night.
Each glance a story yet untold,
A tapestry of warmth and cold.

Silvered Thoughts on Silken Sheets

Draped in whispers, dreams unfold,
Silken threads of tales retold.
Moonlight bathes the room in grace,
As thoughts of you, I softly trace.

Woven memories linger near,
Your laughter bright, your voice so clear.
In this haven, time stands still,
With every breath, my heart you fill.

Starlight's Gentle Caress

Underneath the vast, dark sky,
Stars like diamonds softly lie.
A breeze carries midnight's song,
In this moment, where we belong.

Each twinkle a promise, pure and bright,
Guiding us through the velvet night.
With every heartbeat, magic flows,
In starlight's arms, our love just grows.

Midnight's Embrace

Time slows down in midnight's hold,
A blanket of mystery enfold.
The world outside fades to gray,
In this silence, we drift away.

Softly wrapped in shadows deep,
In this moment, we find our sleep.
With dreams alive, we chase the dawn,
Together in the magic drawn.

Celestial Kaleidoscopes

In the night sky, colors blend,
Vibrant hues that twist and bend.
Stars like jewels, shining bright,
A dance of dreams in the velvet night.

Galaxies swirl in cosmic grace,
Whispers of light in endless space.
Each twinkle tells a story old,
An invitation to the bold.

Through telescopes, we gaze and sigh,
Chasing mysteries in the sky.
Each flicker is a spark divine,
In this vastness, stars align.

Kaleidoscopes of night unfold,
Secrets of the universe untold.
We find ourselves in a cosmic sweep,
In starlit dreams, our spirits leap.

Hidden Threads of Wonder

In the tapestry of life we weave,
Hidden threads that few perceive.
Each moment holds a secret charm,
A gentle touch, a whispered calm.

Underneath the surface lies,
A world alive with unseen ties.
Connections flourish, softly spun,
In the shadows, where dreams run.

Every glance can change a fate,
In little things, we resonate.
The smallest gestures hold such weight,
In silent rooms, we navigate.

Unlocking doors to hidden ways,
In the quiet, wonder stays.
With open hearts, we learn to see,
The beauty in our mystery.

Dancing in Starlight

Beneath the moon, we sway and twirl,
In starlit dreams, our hearts unfurl.
Every note, a spark of grace,
We find our rhythm in this space.

With every breath, the night awakes,
In celestial tides, our spirit shakes.
We spin through shadows, bright and bold,
In dancing light, new stories told.

The universe sways, just like we do,
In cosmic patterns, ever true.
With laughter and joy, our souls ignite,
Dancing freely in the night.

Together we move, hands intertwined,
In the galaxy's embrace, we find.
A symphony whispered in the breeze,
In starlight's sway, our hearts are pleased.

Dreams with Open Eyes

With open eyes, we chase the dawn,
In the vast fields, where dreams are drawn.
Every moment a chance to find,
The beauty nestled in the mind.

Through tangled thoughts, we wander deep,
In the stillness, our visions leap.
Exploring realms where wonders grow,
In waking dreams, our spirits glow.

The world we see is but a spark,
In the shadows, light ignites the dark.
With every heartbeat, stories swell,
In dreams embraced, we know so well.

From whispers soft to thunder loud,
We find our place among the crowd.
With open eyes, we see the skies,
In every step, our spirit flies.

Murmurs from the Ether

Whispers drift on the evening breeze,
Soft secrets carried through rustling leaves.
The stars blink gently, a soothing light,
Guiding lost souls on the edges of night.

Echoes of dreams float in the air,
Velvet notes sing of hope and despair.
A chorus of wishes, a symphony sweet,
Intertwined stories where spirits meet.

Fleeting shadows of memories old,
The warmth of soft voices, a tale to be told.
Under the blanket of twilight's grace,
The universe sighs in this sacred space.

In the murmur of dusk, peace takes flight,
Softly embracing the heart of night.
A dance of the cosmos, vibrant and bright,
In timeless whispers, we find our light.

Fairytale Tides

Upon the shores where dreams collide,
Waves of wonder in a world untied.
Each crest a tale, each foam a song,
Carving magic where we all belong.

Mermaids weave with golden thread,
Stories of love, of journeys ahead.
The ocean whispers, its depths confide,
In every ripple, a fairytale tide.

Stars above in midnight blue,
Guide the heart to what is true.
With every splash, the dreams ignite,
Creating realms in the soft moonlight.

Close your eyes and drift away,
Feel the rhythm come what may.
Each heartbeat follows the ocean's guide,
Lost in the depths of fairytale tides.

Echoes of Comfort

In the stillness where shadows play,
A gentle voice breaks the silence gray.
Whispers of love, solace in tears,
Echoes of comfort dissolve our fears.

Memories linger, soft as a sigh,
Embracing the heart as time rolls by.
With every heartbeat, a story unfolds,
Woven with warmth, a tapestry bold.

Hands intertwined, we face the unknown,
Finding strength in the seeds we've sown.
In moments of doubt, we find our way,
The echoes of comfort forever stay.

Lessons learned from days gone past,
A guiding light, forever steadfast.
In the embrace of memories fond,
Echoes of comfort, a lasting bond.

Glimmers of Serendipity

In the weave of fate, we find our place,
Unexpected journeys, a tender embrace.
Chances taken lead to new skies,
In glimmers of hope, the heart learns to rise.

Every stumble a step towards grace,
In moments of doubt, we find our pace.
Through laughter and tears, we dance and sway,
Glimmers of serendipity guide our way.

The universe twinkles with secrets it keeps,
Timing exact as the world softly sleeps.
In the quiet spaces, dreams interlace,
A spark in the shadows, a life to embrace.

So fear not the twists that life may send,
For every corner turned, there's something to mend.
With open hearts, we journey through,
Glimmers of serendipity shine bright and true.

Dreamy Tidings of Grace

In a realm where shadows play,
Softly glimmers hope's ballet.
Stars weave tales in silver strands,
Guiding souls with gentle hands.

Waves of night embrace the dawn,
Whispers stir as dreams are drawn.
Moments draped in quiet light,
Cradle hearts till morning's flight.

Each heartbeat sings a lullaby,
In the hush where memories lie.
Grace enfolds the weary mind,
In the solace of the kind.

With every breath, new visions soar,
Finding peace on distant shores.
Dreamy tidings softly grace,
Life's sweet moments we embrace.

Twilight's Tender Heart

Twilight casts a golden glow,
As petals fall in soft tableau.
Whispers linger like a sigh,
Painting colors in the sky.

Mountains cradle fading light,
While the stars prepare for flight.
Every heartbeat feels so near,
In this moment, love draws near.

Silhouettes of trees align,
Dancing softly, intertwine.
Tender hearts in twilight's care,
Sharing secrets in the air.

As shadows deepen, dreams unfold,
Each story gently told.
In the dusk, we find our way,
Twilight hearts at close of day.

Whispered Secrets of the Nocturne

Soothe the night with velvet dreams,
Where silence flows in silver streams.
Moonlit echoes softly sigh,
As shadows weave where secrets lie.

Stars alive with ancient tales,
Painting paths where magic sails.
Every whisper, soft and low,
Tells of wonders we don't know.

Crickets sing a lullaby,
In the stillness, time goes by.
Holding close the mysteries,
Floating softly on the breeze.

Cloaked in night's ethereal grace,
Finding peace in this embrace.
Whispered secrets, soft and deep,
In the realm where we can sleep.

Veils of Serenity

Morning breaks with quiet light,
Wrapping dreams in colors bright.
Veils of serenity unfold,
Stories whispered, softly told.

Every breath a gentle sigh,
As the world prepares to fly.
Peaceful moments, tender grace,
Filling hearts in warm embrace.

Gentle waves on shores so near,
Lifting spirits, calming fear.
Nature sings a soothing song,
In her arms, we all belong.

Through the mists, the sun will rise,
Gilding hope in endless skies.
Veils of serenity we seek,
In the silence, soft yet bleak.

A Tapestry Woven with Stardust and Dreams

In the quiet of night,
Stars twinkle bright,
Threads of silver spun,
Woven tales begun.

In the loom of the sky,
Wishes take flight,
With every soft sigh,
Dreams ignite their light.

Patterns of hope dance,
In a cosmic trance,
Embracing the night,
With love's warm advance.

Stardust rains down,
Finding joy in frowns,
A tapestry grand,
Crafted hand in hand.

Luminescent Pathways through the Darkened Realm

Through shadows we tread,
By lanterns we're led,
With each flicker glows,
A path that we chose.

Whispers of the night,
Guide hearts with their light,
A voyage unfolds,
Adventures untold.

Glimmers in the dark,
Each step leaves a mark,
With courage we stand,
In this jeweled land.

Together we roam,
Finding our way home,
In the dance of stars,
Healing all our scars.

Twilight's Gift of Enchanted Whispers

As daylight retreats,
Twilight softly greets,
With secrets unfurled,
A magical world.

Whispers ride the breeze,
Through the swaying trees,
Promises of the night,
In shadows take flight.

Stars begin to sing,
Of dreams on the wing,
Echoes of delight,
In the hush of night.

With each passing hour,
We embrace the power,
Of twilight's sweet grace,
In this sacred space.

Whispers of Nightlight

In the still of the night,
Flickering sights,
Gentle luminescence,
Guides our existence.

From the moon's soft glow,
Soft secrets bestow,
Tales of ancient lore,
On the midnight shore.

Echoes softly weave,
In hearts that believe,
With nightlight's embrace,
We find our true place.

Whispers dance around,
In dreams we are found,
With the stars up high,
We learn how to fly.

Ethereal Pathways

Whispers ride the morning breeze,
Through the trees, they dance with ease.
Footsteps on the dewy grass,
Time slows down, moments pass.

Light filters through the branches wide,
Nature's secrets, hearts confide.
Paths unseen, yet deeply felt,
On this journey, worries melt.

In the hush, a sacred tune,
Beneath the watchful, glowing moon.
Every stone and every bough,
Lead to where we're meant to bow.

Ethereal pathways, guiding dreams,
In the stillness, life redeems.
With each step, we find our way,
In this dance, forever stay.

Shadows of Wonder

Underneath the starlit sky,
Mysteries linger, never shy.
Shadows play on ancient ground,
Echoes of the past resound.

Flickering flames in the night,
Stories told in flickered light.
Whispers of a world unknown,
Secrets in the dusk are sown.

Glimmers of hope, shadows cast,
In this moment, truth held fast.
A labyrinth of dreams we find,
In the darkness, hearts entwined.

Shadows dance, a wondrous play,
Guiding souls along the way.
Lift your gaze, embrace the dark,
In every shadow, there's a spark.

Nights Painted in Gold

Painted skies with hues so bright,
Every constellation ignites.
A tapestry of dreams unfolds,
Wrapped in warmth, nights painted in gold.

Whispers of the evening breeze,
Crickets sing among the trees.
Golden dreams in twilight's fold,
Stories waiting to be told.

Moments shared, a gentle touch,
In the quiet, it means so much.
Stars like jewels, a soft embrace,
In every heartbeat, find your place.

Nights painted in gold, we soar,
Chasing dreams, longing for more.
Together under heaven's dome,
In this magic, we find home.

Floating on Soft Currents

Gentle waves beneath the sun,
Flowing freely, we are one.
Floating on soft currents, light,
Follow paths of pure delight.

Raindrops dance on tranquil seas,
Nature's melody, sweet as breeze.
Hearts unbound by earthly chains,
In this moment, joy remains.

Clouds above, a drifting song,
In this realm, we all belong.
With each breath, we feel the flow,
Floating high, transcending low.

Soft currents cradle every dream,
In the light, we gently beam.
Let the waters guide our heart,
In this journey, we won't part.

Ethereal Slumbers

In twilight's hush, the dreamers sigh,
Soft whispers dance in the night sky.
Stars flicker softly, like tender beams,
Wrapping the world in silken dreams.

Moonlight casts shadows, playful and deep,
Cradling the earth as it drifts to sleep.
Gentle breezes weave through the trees,
Here, in slumber, we find our peace.

Each breath a lull, each heartbeat a song,
In this quiet realm, we all belong.
Ethereal visions, like mist they glide,
In this sacred space, we all can hide.

Dappled Light on Feathery Clouds

Sunlight peeks through soft, white veil,
Whispers of warmth, a gentle trail.
Dappled light plays on the ground,
In this serene space, joy is found.

Clouds like cotton, drifting so high,
Painting the canvas of a clear sky.
Moments of wonder, fleeting yet bright,
Dappled light dances, pure delight.

Nature's embrace, both tender and wide,
Shelters our hearts where dreams can bide.
In feathery clouds, our spirits rise,
Awash in a sea of endless skies.

Serene Visions in the Dark

In the stillness, shadows breathe,
Secrets whispered, the night weaves.
Serene visions bloom and fade,
In the dark, dreams are laid.

Stars like diamonds, cold and bright,
Guide the wanderers through the night.
Calm reflections stir the soul,
In the dark, we become whole.

The moon's embrace, a silvery glow,
Illuminating paths we do not know.
In tranquil waters, thoughts do glide,
Serene visions, our trusted guide.

Illumined Thoughts of Midnight

Midnight whispers, the clock's soft chime,
Illumined thoughts, lost in time.
The world is hushed, dreams take flight,
In this sacred hour, all feels right.

Stars ignite with stories untold,
Shimmering futures, daring and bold.
Each flicker a spark of hope anew,
Illumined thoughts, they guide us through.

In the heart of night, ideas bloom,
Casting away the shadows of gloom.
With every breath, we create and share,
Illumined thoughts, forever rare.

Floating into the Ether

In the quiet of the night,
Whispers dance upon the breeze,
Carried far from earthly sights,
Into realms where thoughts find ease.

Stars above wink with their light,
Guiding dreams that drift and sway,
Lifting souls to endless heights,
Where the heart can freely play.

Clouds like ships on oceans roam,
Sailing through a velvet sea,
In this space, we find our home,
Floating into what we could be.

With each breath, we leave behind,
Fears that once held us confined,
In the ether, we unwind,
Together, souls intertwined.

Shadows of the Heart

In the corners where silence dwells,
Whispers echo of love's sweet pain,
Shadows linger, weaving spells,
In memories, we find the rain.

Moments captured in twilight's hue,
Faint reminders of what we've lost,
Yet in the dark, there's a glimmer too,
A warmth that defies the bitter cost.

Each heartbeat carries tales of yore,
Of laughter shared and tears released,
In this dance, we seek for more,
Finding solace where fears ceased.

Though shadows may obscure the light,
Hope remains a guiding spark,
With love's embrace, we chase the night,
Finding strength within the dark.

Lanterns of Serene Thought

Upon the lake, reflections glow,
Lanterns floating, soft and bright,
Casting dreams as gentle flow,
Guiding minds through tranquil night.

In every flicker, peace unfolds,
Echoing the heart's deep sigh,
Stories whispered, softly told,
As the stars embrace the sky.

Thoughts like petals drift away,
Tossed upon the evening's breath,
In their dance, we find our way,
Letting go of worry's heft.

With each lantern, hope ignites,
A path illuminated wide,
In serene thought, our future lights,
Together, let our hearts abide.

Stardust Embrace

In the hush of endless night,
We gather dreams like stardust fine,
Kissed by light, we take our flight,
Wrapped in magic, yours and mine.

Whirling through the cosmic flow,
Galaxies of hopes unfurled,
In this moment, we both know,
We are stardust in this world.

Hearts entwined like constellations,
Drawing maps of love's design,
With each pulse, we form creations,
A tapestry of spark divine.

So let us dance in cosmic grace,
With every wish, let spirits rise,
In the universe, we find our place,
Forever held in stardust skies.

Velvet Nights and Stardust Wishes

In velvet nights where whispers play,
Stars twinkle softly, lighting the way.
Dreams drift gently on moonlit streams,
Wrapped in the warmth of starlit dreams.

Wishes flutter like fireflies bright,
Painting the dark with sparkling light.
Each secret shared beneath the sky,
Echoes of hope as the night drifts by.

A tapestry woven from silken sighs,
Time dances softly as moments rise.
Holding these treasures so close and dear,
Velvet nights cradle our every fear.

In stillness we find what hearts can seek,
Magic unfolds in the silence we speak.
Stardust wishes, a soft serenade,
Under the stars, our dreams are made.

Shadows of the Dreamer

In shadows cast by the fleeting day,
The dreamer wanders, lost in the sway.
Whispers of night cradle hope so sweet,
Softly echoing in the heart's heartbeat.

Between the realms of dusk and dawn,
A world awakens, still yet withdrawn.
Each shadow speaks of stories untold,
In the glow of the moon, secrets unfold.

Tender and fragile, the night carries dreams,
Illuminating paths on silver beams.
With every heartbeat, the dreams come alive,
In shadows of twilight, the spirits thrive.

The dance of the stars in a velvety sea,
Guides all the dreamers who long to be free.
In the soft embrace of the night's gentle shroud,
Shadows of hope gather, silent yet loud.

Luminescent Fantasies

In wild gardens where colors collide,
Luminescent dreams in night's gentle tide.
Fantasies bloom with the softest of light,
Painting the world in the hush of the night.

Each whispering leaf, a tale to impart,
Echoes of wonder that dwell in the heart.
Time sways like petals in a playful breeze,
Carrying magic with effortless ease.

Through glimmers and sparkles, the moments entwine,
Weaving a story that's yours and that's mine.
In the canvas of night where our spirits take flight,
Luminescent fantasies brighten the night.

Here in this realm where all dreams intertwine,
Secrets unravel like delicate twine.
Under the glow of our hearts, we embark,
Fantasies dance in the light through the dark.

Silhouettes Under the Stars

In the hush of the night, we stand hand in hand,
Silhouettes swaying, following the sand.
Stars above sparkle like eyes in the dark,
Whispers of love, a soft, tender spark.

Each shadow entwined, our stories unfold,
Moments of warmth in the night's gentle hold.
The breeze carries secrets from far and wide,
As we share our dreams with the night as our guide.

Beneath the vast sky where wishes take flight,
Silhouettes linger, embracing the night.
In the magic of starlight, we find our way,
Together forever, come what may.

Hand in hand, we traverse the unknown,
Under the cosmos, our spirits have grown.
Silhouettes of lovers in the softest embrace,
Under the stars, we've found our place.

Radiant Glimmers in the Midnight Sky

Stars twinkle bright in the dark,
Whispers of dreams yet to embark.
Moonlight dances on the stream,
Casting shadows, a silver beam.

Night blooms softly, secrets unfold,\nEach glimmer a story retold.
The cosmos sighs in silent grace,
Embracing all in its vast space.

Galaxies swirl in cosmic flight,
Painting wonders in the night.
Timeless tales woven in air,
Starlit wishes, hopes laid bare.

A canvas of night, ever wide,
Where nightingales and dreams abide.
In every glimmer, a spark, a sigh,
Radiant whispers in the sky.

Ethereal Echoes of Nighttime Reverie

In the hush of twilight's call,
Dreams take shape, and shadows fall.
A melody hums through the trees,
Carried gently by the breeze.

The moon casts its enchanting glow,
A silver path where wishes flow.
Reflections dance on tranquil lakes,
In every ripple, a heartbeat wakes.

Tonight, the stars begin to weave,
Tales of magic for us to believe.
Each echo a promise from afar,
Wrapped in the light of a distant star.

With every sigh, the night delights,
As echoes join in silent flights.
Ethereal whispers fill the air,
Leaving traces of dreams everywhere.

Slumber's Serenade Under the Cosmic Canopy

Lullabies drift in soft embrace,
Under the night's tender grace.
Stars hum sweetly in their sleep,
Guardians of secrets we can keep.

Clouds swirl like whispers, so light,
Cradling dreams in the still of night.
Each twinkle a note in the air,
Serenading souls everywhere.

Slumber's dance weaves tales untold,
In realms of night's soft and bold.
Awakening hearts in a gentle way,
Embraced by the stars until the day.

Underneath the cosmic dome,
Every dream finds its way home.
A serenade for those who rest,
In the arms of night, forever blessed.

Wistful Wanderings Through Celestial Shadows

Beyond the stars, the visions roam,
In twilight's arms, they find a home.
Wanderers drift through shadowed paths,
Where every step whispers math.

Light and dark in a gentle dance,
Creating a world of sweet romance.
With each heartbeat, our wishes fly,
Through celestial shadows, we dare to try.

Echoes of starlight guide our way,
Turning dusk into a brighter day.
In the folds of night, we dream and yearn,
For the stories of stars, we eternally learn.

Wistful journeys, souls align,
Chasing shadows, hearts entwine.
In the silence, we find our truth,
In the cosmos' embrace, we reclaim our youth.

Crystalline Whispers

In the quiet night, they gleam,
Soft reflections on a stream.
Whispers dance on wind's embrace,
Secrets shared in sacred space.

Frosted branches, silver bright,
Capturing the moon's pure light.
Silent songs, in shadows' play,
Nature's breath, a soft ballet.

Glistening flakes that fall like tears,
Holding dreams of fleeting years.
Crystal visions, bright and clear,
Echoes drawing ever near.

In the dawn, they fade away,
Leaving just a hint of play.
Yet in hearts, they'll always stay,
Whispers of the night's ballet.

Celestial Hiding Places

Stars twinkle in velvet skies,
Where the ancient silence lies.
Nestled deep in cosmic glow,
Secrets only starlight knows.

Nebulae, soft clouds of dreams,
Whispers wrapped in twilight beams.
Galaxies in playful chase,
In the dark, their hiding place.

Planets spin in quiet dance,
Caught in time's eternal trance.
A symphony of light and shade,
Tales of love and grace displayed.

In the night, we search for truth,
In the cosmos, time uncouth.
For in these vast, celestial schemes,
Lie the hidden hopes and dreams.

Night-Woven Tales

Beneath the veil of shadowed skies,
Whispers weave with soft replies.
Moonlit paths that twine and curl,
Stories dance and gently swirl.

Owls sing songs of olden lore,
Each hoot opens an ancient door.
In the stillness, echoes flow,
Tales of heartache, joy, and woe.

Stars above lend their bright gaze,
Illuminating night's soft maze.
Fables told in silken threads,
Crafting dreams in quiet beds.

Hold the magic, pause the time,
In the night, all seems sublime.
For each tale that shadows read,
Blooms within like a night's seed.

Twilight's Cartographer

On the edge of day and night,
Where colors fuse and hearts take flight.
Mapping moments, soft and bright,
In the hue of fading light.

Brushstrokes blend on canvas wide,
Shadows linger, hopes abide.
Golden rays in twilight's hand,
Sketch the dreams across the land.

Every breath a dotted line,
Guiding souls through space and time.
With each heartbeat, charts unfold,
Stories waiting to be told.

In twilight's glow, the world is free,
A cartographer of destiny.
As dusk unfurls its tapestry,
Mapping dreams for you and me.

Celestial Embrace of the Dreamer

In the quiet glow of night,
Dreamers weave their soft light.
Stars whisper secrets from afar,
Guiding hearts like a distant star.

With eyes closed, visions ignite,
Floating through the cosmic sight.
Every wish a shooting flame,
In this realm, we find our name.

Echoes dance on velvet skies,
Filling souls with sweet reprise.
Time stands still, the world a blur,
In dreams, our hearts gently stir.

Wrapped in stardust, pure delight,
The dreamer's heart takes wondrous flight.
Forever held in cosmic grace,
In this embrace, we find our place.

Murmurs of a Starry Night

The night unfolds in silken hues,
Each star a whisper, a gentle muse.
Softly cradled by the moon's light,
We journey through this starry night.

Crickets chirp a lullaby tune,
As shadows dance beneath the moon.
The sky adorned with twinkling dreams,
In silence, we hear the night's themes.

Each constellation tells a tale,
Of lovers lost or ships that sail.
In the stillness, hearts ignite,
By the murmurs of the night.

A tapestry of twinkling eyes,
Where wishes are sewn in midnight sighs.
Together we wander, spirits bright,
Forever bound by this starry night.

Fragile Threads of Midnight

Underneath the haunting glow,
Fragile threads of dreams bestow.
Weaving wishes into the air,
Midnight's beauty, soft and rare.

Each moment spun with tender care,
A dance of hope, a secret prayer.
Gently wandering through the dark,
Tracing paths where shadows spark.

Delicate as whispers shared,
In the silence, hearts prepared.
Flickering like a candle's light,
Guiding souls through starry night.

With every breath, the threads entwine,
A tapestry of love divine.
In the embrace of the quiet tide,
Our fragile dreams shall not subside.

Where Wishes Take Flight

Beneath the arch of velvet skies,
Wishes flutter, unbound, they rise.
Carried high on zephyr's breath,
Each hope a spark, defying death.

In the soft glow of dawn's embrace,
Promises dance in fleeting grace.
Every dream a feathered kite,
Soaring onward, taking flight.

With hearts unchained, we chase the light,
In the garden where wishes ignite.
Boundless journeys begin anew,
In the realm where dreams come true.

Through valleys deep and mountains high,
We find our wings, we learn to fly.
Together woven, spirits bright,
This is where our wishes take flight.

The Secret Life of Stars in Dreamscapes

In hidden realms where shadows play,
Stars dance softly, night turns to day.
Their secrets whispered on cosmic breeze,
With dreams enfolding, hearts find ease.

Glittering tales of ancient lore,
Shimmering lights forever soar.
A symphony of magic spun,
In night's embrace, the dreams are won.

Beneath the gaze of silver beams,
We wander lost in silver dreams.
Each twinkle spins a different tale,
Where hearts can soar, where hopes prevail.

In realms of stardust, we unite,
And lose ourselves in endless night.
With every blink, a wish takes flight,
In secret life, we find the light.

Reflections of Light in a Sleepy Haven

In pastel hues, the morning gleams,
Soft sunlight spills, it gently seems.
On lakes like mirrors, dreams are cast,
A sleepy haven, pure and vast.

Tender whispers from the trees,
Embrace the calm, a soft-edged breeze.
Reflections shimmer, time stands still,
A secret world, serene and chill.

Where shadows play with hues of gold,
The stories of the day unfold.
In restless hearts, a quiet wish,
For moments wrapped in silken bliss.

As echoes flutter with a beat,
This haven hums, so soft and sweet.
In hands of time, we gently sway,
In sleepy light, we drift away.

Whispers of the Universe in Quiet Moments

In quiet moments, silence sings,
Whispers float on gentle wings.
The universe speaks in quiet tones,
In stillness, we uncover our own.

Stars beckon softly from afar,
Guiding dreams like a glowing star.
With cosmic grace, our thoughts take flight,
As whispers weave through endless night.

Time unfolds like a delicate thread,
In tranquil hours, all words are said.
Through heartbeats shared, the cosmos sways,
In whispered truths, our spirit plays.

Among the shadows, light will flow,
In sacred spaces, feel the glow.
The universe stretches, wide and free,
In quiet moments, just you and me.

Eternal Horizons of Fantasy's Embrace

Upon the horizon, dreams take form,
In fantasy's grasp, the heart is warm.
With skies of wonder and seas of light,
Eternal horizons promise flight.

Imaginary realms where we explore,
A treasure trove behind each door.
In vivid hues, our wishes bloom,
The heart ignites, dispelling gloom.

From peaks of dreams, we gaze within,
Chasing the magic; let the journey begin.
With every heartbeat, each step we trace,
In fantasy's arms, we find our place.

Together we sail on a whispering breeze,
To worlds unseen, through twilight trees.
In this dance of fate, we share a grace,
In eternal horizons, we find our space.

Soft Serenades of Slumber

In the quiet night, whispers play,
Moonlight spills, soft and gray.
Gentle breezes weave through trees,
Singing secrets with the breeze.

Dreams float lightly, like feathers fall,
Crickets serenade, a soothing call.
Stars blink softly, a lullaby,
Embracing hearts, as time drifts by.

Rest your head, let worries fade,
In this peace, sweet dreams are laid.
Close your eyes, let the night unfold,
In soft serenades, warmth to hold.

Morning whispers, gentle and bright,
Awakens softly, the end of night.
Yet in your heart, the echoes stay,
Of soft serenades that softly play.

Starlit Hushes

The night sky glimmers, calm and deep,
In starlit hushes, the world does sleep.
Clouds drift slowly, a velvet sea,
Wrapped in shadows, so wild and free.

Moonbeams dance on the silver grass,
Whispers echo, as moments pass.
Nature sighs in a tranquil tune,
Beneath the watchful, glowing moon.

Dreams take flight on a night so clear,
In starlit hushes, all is near.
Crickets chant in a soft refrain,
As sleepy stars begin to wane.

A gentle night that breathes and sways,
In the starlit hush, peace always stays.
Hold this moment close, dear and tight,
For these are gifts from the night.

Lullabies Beneath the Cosmos

Under the heavens, vast and wide,
Lullabies whisper, the stars confide.
Galaxies twinkle with secrets bright,
As dreams take flight on this quiet night.

Softly, the world drifts into calm,
Wrapped in a night that feels like balm.
The universe hums a soothing song,
In this embrace, we all belong.

Clouds gather softly, a blanket of gray,
In lullabies sung, worries fray.
Beneath the cosmos, hearts gently sway,
As night unfolds, and dreams come to play.

Each star a promise, each moonbeam a kiss,
Wrapped in the magic, we find our bliss.
In lullabies sweet, the world fades away,
Vowing to meet when the night turns to day.

Dreams in the Silver Glow

In silver glow, the world is hushed,
Time stands still, in silence brushed.
Soft shadows dance on the wooden floor,
Opening dreams, beckoning more.

Whispers of night wrapped in delight,
Carry us gently into the night.
The moonlight plays on our sleepy eyes,
As dreams unfurl like a painted sky.

Each heartbeat echoes a tender sigh,
In the silver glow, we learn to fly.
Floating on wishes, shy and bright,
Lost in the wonder of this sweet night.

With every moment, the stars will spin,
Awakening dreams wrapped deep within.
In the silver glow, we'll rest, and flow,
As dreams come alive in the night's soft show.

Astral Visions Beneath Velvet Skies

Stars twinkle softly, whispers bright,
Dreams take flight in the silence of night.
Constellations weave tales of old,
In cosmic embrace, our secrets unfold.

Moonlight dances on tranquil streams,
Silhouettes reflect our slumbering dreams.
Beneath velvet skies, magic begins,
In the stillness where wonder wins.

Galaxies spin in a hazy embrace,
Each moment captured, time leaves no trace.
We lose ourselves in the vast unknown,
Every heartbeat sings of dreams overblown.

Floating on whispers of celestial sound,
In astral visions, our hopes are unbound.
With every sigh, the universe sighs,
As we chase the stars beneath velvet skies.

Echoes of Serenity in the Night Air

A gentle breeze carries secrets untold,
Through the quiet night, where dreams unfold.
The moon's soft glow, a beacon so clear,
Echoes of serenity, drawing us near.

Crickets sing softly, a soothing refrain,
In the heart of the night, there's peace from the pain.
Stars glisten like diamonds on a velvet sea,
Awakening whispers of who we can be.

Each moment lingers, wrapped in the light,
In echoes of kindness, hearts take flight.
The world fades away, lost in its charm,
In the calm of the night, we find healing balm.

Let us breathe deeply, embrace the still,
In the night's tender arms, we feel the thrill.
With every heartbeat, we cherish this prayer,
In echoes of serenity, floating through air.

Conversations with the Night's Gentle Caress

Underneath the stars, stories unfold,
The night whispers gently, secrets of old.
In shadows we linger, hearts intertwined,
Conversations with night, where dreams are aligned.

The cool breeze that carries sweet lullabies,
Invites us to listen with wide, open eyes.
We speak with the moon, and the stars reply,
In shimmering silence, our spirits can fly.

Every heartbeat counts as shadows dance close,
In the arms of the night, we let ourselves coast.
In twilight's embrace, we find our true self,
Conversations with night, a treasure, our wealth.

As dawn slowly breaks, we sigh in content,
For the night's gentle caress feels heaven-sent.
In memories woven with silver and gold,
Conversations linger, forever retold.

Resting on a Galaxy's Edge

Upon the edge of a galaxy's light,
We lay on the stardust, lost in the night.
The cosmos hums softly, a lullaby sweet,
In the vastness of space, we find our heartbeat.

Nebulas swirl in a dance of pure grace,
Whispering secrets, we're part of this space.
With each gentle pulse, the universe talks,
As we rest on the edge, where time gently walks.

Planets adrift in their orbits so deep,
Cradle our dreams, as the heavens keep.
We wander in silence, our thoughts intertwine,
In this cosmic embrace, your heart next to mine.

Forever we linger, in this celestial dance,
Where starlight and shadows ignite a romance.
Resting on fringes of galaxies wide,
In the unseen magic where love can abide.